Guest Book to Celebrate

_____

_____

Event Date

_____

THANK YOU FOR COMING.

Let's celebrate!

Guest Name

_____

Thoughts & Messages

_____

_____

_____

_____

_____

_____

EMAIL/PHONE

_____

Guest Name

_____

Thoughts & Messages

_____

_____

_____

_____

_____

_____

✉ Email/Phone
_____

Guest Name

_____

Thoughts & Messages

_____

_____

_____

_____

_____

_____

_____

Email/Phone _____

Guest Name

_____

Thoughts & Messages

_____

_____

_____

_____

_____

_____

EMAIL/PHONE _____

Guest Name

Thoughts & Messages

_____

_____

_____

_____

_____

_____

EMAIL/PHONE _____

Guest Name

_____

Thoughts & Messages

_____

_____

_____

_____

_____

_____

_____

EMAIL/PHONE _____

Guest Name

_____

Thoughts & Messages

_____

_____

_____

_____

_____

_____

EMAIL/PHONE _____

Guest Name

Thoughts & Messages

Guest Name

_____

Thoughts & Messages

_____

_____

_____

_____

_____

_____

_____

EMAIL/PHONE _____

Guest Name

_____

Thoughts & Messages

_____

_____

_____

_____

_____

_____

EMAIL/PHONE _____

Guest Name

_____

Thoughts & Messages

_____

_____

_____

_____

_____

_____

EMAIL/PHONE _____

Guest Name

_____

Thoughts & Messages

_____

_____

_____

_____

_____

_____

_____

EMAIL/PHONE
_____

Guest Name

_____

Thoughts & Messages

_____

_____

_____

_____

_____

_____

EMAIL/PHONE _____

Guest Name

_____

Thoughts & Messages

_____

_____

_____

_____

_____

_____

_____

EMAIL/PHONE _____

Guest Name

_____

Thoughts & Messages

_____

_____

_____

_____

_____

_____

EMAIL/PHONE _____

Guest Name

_____

Thoughts & Messages

_____

_____

_____

_____

_____

_____

_____

EMAIL/PHONE _____

Guest Name

_____

Thoughts & Messages

_____

_____

_____

_____

_____

_____

_____

EMAIL/PHONE _____

Guest Name

_____

Thoughts & Messages

_____

_____

_____

_____

_____

_____

_____

EMAIL/PHONE _____

Guest Name

Thoughts & Messages

Email/Phone

Guest Name

_____

Thoughts & Messages

_____

_____

_____

_____

_____

_____

_____

EMAIL/PHONE

Guest Name

Thoughts & Messages

Email/Phone

Guest Name

_____

Thoughts & Messages

_____

_____

_____

_____

_____

_____

✉

EMAIL/PHONE _____

Guest Name

Thoughts & Messages

_____

_____

_____

_____

_____

_____

_____

EMAIL/PHONE _____

Guest Name

_____

Thoughts & Messages

_____

_____

_____

_____

_____

_____

_____

EMAIL/PHONE
_____

Guest Name

Thoughts & Messages

Email/Phone

Guest Name

_____

Thoughts & Messages

_____

_____

_____

_____

_____

_____

_____

Email/Phone _____

Guest Name

_____

Thoughts & Messages

_____

_____

_____

_____

_____

_____

_____

EMAIL/PHONE _____

Guest Name

_____

Thoughts & Messages

_____

_____

_____

_____

_____

_____

_____

EMAIL/PHONE _____

Guest Name

_____

Thoughts & Messages

_____

_____

_____

_____

_____

_____

_____

EMAIL/PHONE _____

Guest Name

_____

Thoughts & Messages

_____

_____

_____

_____

_____

_____

_____

✉ E

EMAIL/PHONE _____

Guest Name

_____

Thoughts & Messages

_____

_____

_____

_____

_____

_____

EMAIL/PHONE _____

Guest Name

_____

Thoughts & Messages

_____

_____

_____

_____

_____

_____

Email/Phone _____

Guest Name

Thoughts & Messages

_____

_____

_____

_____

_____

_____

_____

EMAIL/PHONE _____

Guest Name

_____

Thoughts & Messages

_____

_____

_____

_____

_____

_____

EMAIL/PHONE
_____

Guest Name

_____

Thoughts & Messages

_____

_____

_____

_____

_____

_____

Email/Phone _____

Guest Name

_____

Thoughts & Messages

_____

_____

_____

_____

_____

_____

EMAIL/PHONE _____

Guest Name

_____

Thoughts & Messages

_____

_____

_____

_____

_____

_____

_____

EMAIL/PHONE _____

Guest Name

_____

Thoughts & Messages

_____

_____

_____

_____

_____

_____

_____

EMAIL/PHONE _____

Guest Name

Thoughts & Messages

Email/Phone
_____

Guest Name

_____

Thoughts & Messages

_____

_____

_____

_____

_____

_____

EMAIL/PHONE _____

Guest Name

_____

Thoughts & Messages

_____

_____

_____

_____

_____

_____

_____

EMAIL/PHONE _____

Guest Name

_____

Thoughts & Messages

_____

_____

_____

_____

_____

_____

EMAIL/PHONE _____

Guest Name

Thoughts & Messages

Email/Phone

Guest Name

_____

Thoughts & Messages

_____

_____

_____

_____

_____

_____

_____

EMAIL/PHONE _____

Guest Name

_____

Thoughts & Messages

_____

_____

_____

_____

_____

_____

_____

EMAIL/PHONE _____

Guest Name

_____

Thoughts & Messages

_____

_____

_____

_____

_____

_____

EMAIL/PHONE _____

Guest Name

_____

Thoughts & Messages

_____

_____

_____

_____

_____

_____

_____

Email/Phone _____

Guest Name

_____

Thoughts & Messages

_____

_____

_____

_____

_____

_____

_____

Email/Phone _____

Guest Name

_____

Thoughts & Messages

_____

_____

_____

_____

_____

_____

Email/Phone _____

Guest Name

_____

Thoughts & Messages

_____

_____

_____

_____

_____

_____

EMAIL/PHONE _____

Guest Name

_____

Thoughts & Messages

_____

_____

_____

_____

_____

_____

_____

Email/Phone _____

Guest Name

_____

Thoughts & Messages

_____

_____

_____

_____

_____

_____

Email/Phone
_____

Guest Name

_____

Thoughts & Messages

_____

_____

_____

_____

_____

_____

_____

Email/Phone _____

Guest Name

_____

Thoughts & Messages

_____

_____

_____

_____

_____

_____

EMAIL/PHONE _____

Guest Name

_____

Thoughts & Messages

_____

_____

_____

_____

_____

_____

_____

EMAIL/PHONE _____

Guest Name

_____

Thoughts & Messages

_____

_____

_____

_____

_____

_____

EMAIL/PHONE _____

Guest Name

_____

Thoughts & Messages

_____

_____

_____

_____

_____

_____

_____

EMAIL/PHONE _____

Guest Name

_____

Thoughts & Messages

_____

_____

_____

_____

_____

_____

_____

EMAIL/PHONE _____

Guest Name

Thoughts & Messages

_____

_____

_____

_____

_____

_____

_____

EMAIL/PHONE _____

Guest Name

_____

Thoughts & Messages

_____

_____

_____

_____

_____

_____

EMAIL/PHONE _____

Guest Name

Thoughts & Messages

Email/Phone

Guest Name

_____

Thoughts & Messages

_____

_____

_____

_____

_____

_____

EMAIL/PHONE _____

Guest Name

Thoughts & Messages

EMAIL/PHONE

Guest Name

_____

Thoughts & Messages

_____

_____

_____

_____

_____

_____

_____

EMAIL/PHONE _____

Guest Name

_____

Thoughts & Messages

_____

_____

_____

_____

_____

_____

_____

EMAIL/PHONE _____

Guest Name

_____

Thoughts & Messages

_____

_____

_____

_____

_____

_____

_____

Email/Phone _____

Guest Name

_____

Thoughts & Messages

_____

_____

_____

_____

_____

_____

_____

EMAIL/PHONE _____

Guest Name

_____

Thoughts & Messages

_____

_____

_____

_____

_____

_____

EMAIL/PHONE _____

Guest Name

_____

Thoughts & Messages

_____

_____

_____

_____

_____

_____

_____

EMAIL/PHONE _____

Guest Name

_____

Thoughts & Messages

_____

_____

_____

_____

_____

_____

_____

EMAIL/PHONE _____

Guest Name

_____

Thoughts & Messages

_____

_____

_____

_____

_____

_____

Email/Phone
_____

Guest Name

_____

Thoughts & Messages

_____

_____

_____

_____

_____

_____

EMAIL/PHONE _____

Guest Name

_____

Thoughts & Messages

_____

_____

_____

_____

_____

_____

_____

EMAIL/PHONE _____

Guest Name

_____

Thoughts & Messages

_____

_____

_____

_____

_____

_____

_____

EMAIL/PHONE _____

Guest Name

_____

Thoughts & Messages

_____

_____

_____

_____

_____

_____

_____

EMAIL/PHONE _____

Guest Name

_____

Thoughts & Messages

_____

_____

_____

_____

_____

_____

EMAIL/PHONE _____

Guest Name

Thoughts & Messages

_____

_____

_____

_____

_____

_____

_____

Email/Phone _____

Guest Name

_____

Thoughts & Messages

_____

_____

_____

_____

_____

_____

_____

EMAIL/PHONE _____

Guest Name

_____

Thoughts & Messages

_____

_____

_____

_____

_____

_____

EMAIL/PHONE _____

Guest Name

_____

Thoughts & Messages

_____

_____

_____

_____

_____

_____

_____

EMAIL/PHONE _____

Guest Name

_____

Thoughts & Messages

_____

_____

_____

_____

_____

_____

_____

EMAIL/PHONE _____

Guest Name

Thoughts & Messages

✉ Email/Phone

Guest Name

_____

Thoughts & Messages

_____

_____

_____

_____

_____

_____

_____

EMAIL/PHONE _____

Guest Name

_____

Thoughts & Messages

_____

_____

_____

_____

_____

_____

EMAIL/PHONE _____

Guest Name

_____

Thoughts & Messages

_____

_____

_____

_____

_____

_____

Email/Phone _____

Guest Name

_____

Thoughts & Messages

_____

_____

_____

_____

_____

_____

_____

✉ E

EMAIL/PHONE _____

Guest Name

_____

Thoughts & Messages

_____

_____

_____

_____

_____

_____

EMAIL/PHONE _____

Guest Name

_____

Thoughts & Messages

_____

_____

_____

_____

_____

_____

_____

EMAIL/PHONE _____

Guest Name

_____

Thoughts & Messages

_____

_____

_____

_____

_____

_____

Email/Phone _____

Guest Name

_____

Thoughts & Messages

_____

_____

_____

_____

_____

_____

_____

✉ E

EMAIL/PHONE _____

Guest Name

_____

Thoughts & Messages

_____

_____

_____

_____

_____

_____

_____

EMAIL/PHONE _____

Guest Name

_____

Thoughts & Messages

_____

_____

_____

_____

_____

_____

_____

EMAIL/PHONE
_____

Guest Name

_____

Thoughts & Messages

_____

_____

_____

_____

_____

_____

_____

Email/Phone _____

Guest Name

_____

Thoughts & Messages

_____

_____

_____

_____

_____

_____

_____

EMAIL/PHONE _____

Guest Name

_____

Thoughts & Messages

_____

_____

_____

_____

_____

_____

EMAIL/PHONE _____

Guest Name

_____

Thoughts & Messages

_____

_____

_____

_____

_____

_____

_____

EMAIL/PHONE _____

Guest Name

_____

Thoughts & Messages

_____

_____

_____

_____

_____

_____

_____

Email/Phone _____

Guest Name

_____

Thoughts & Messages

_____

_____

_____

_____

_____

_____

_____

EMAIL/PHONE
_____

Guest Name

_____

Thoughts & Messages

_____

_____

_____

_____

_____

_____

_____

EMAIL/PHONE _____

Guest Name

_____

Thoughts & Messages

_____

_____

_____

_____

_____

_____

✉ Email/Phone _____

Guest Name

_____

Thoughts & Messages

_____

_____

_____

_____

_____

_____

Email/Phone _____

Guest Name

_____

Thoughts & Messages

_____

_____

_____

_____

_____

_____

_____

✉ E

EMAIL/PHONE
_____

Guest Name

_____

Thoughts & Messages

_____

_____

_____

_____

_____

_____

_____

EMAIL/PHONE _____

Guest Name

_____

Thoughts & Messages

_____

_____

_____

_____

_____

_____

Email/Phone _____

Guest Name

_____

Thoughts & Messages

_____

_____

_____

_____

_____

_____

EMAIL/PHONE _____

NOTES & PHOTOS

NOTES & PHOTOS

NOTES & PHOTOS

NOTES & PHOTOS

NOTES & PHOTOS

GIFT LOG

Name / Email / Phone	Gift

GIFT LOG

Name /Email /Phone   **Gift**

_____   _____

_____   _____

_____   _____

_____   _____

_____   _____

_____   _____

_____   _____

_____   _____

_____   _____

_____   _____

_____   _____

_____   _____

GIFT LOG

Name /Email /Phone	Gift

GIFT LOG

Name / Email / Phone	Gift

GIFT LOG

Name / Email / Phone	Gift

GIFT LOG

Name /Email /Phone	Gift

GIFT LOG

Name / Email / Phone	Gift

CPSIA information can be obtained
at www.ICGtesting.com
Printed in the USA
BVHW051310230920
589453BV00014B/843